10 Minutes a Day

Times Tables

for ages 5-7

This CGP book is bursting with quick
Times Tables activities for children aged 5-7.

Plus, it's packed with colourful stickers so they'll have
fun while they're learning all the essential skills!

Contents

Counting in 2s 2

Groups of 2 3

2 Times Table 4

More 2 Times Table 5

2 Times Table Facts 6

More 2 Times Table Facts 7

Mixed 2 Times Table 8

Counting in 5s 9

Groups of 5 10

5 Times Table 11

More 5 Times Table 12

5 Times Table Facts 13

More 5 Times Table Facts 14

Mixed 5 Times Table 15

Counting in 10s 16

Groups of 10 17

10 Times Table 18

More 10 Times Table 19

10 Times Table Facts 20

More 10 Times Table Facts 21

Mixed 10 Times Table 22

Counting in 2s, 5s and 10s 23

Groups of 2, 5 and 10 24

Mixed 2 and 10 Times Tables ... 25

Mixed 5 and 10 Times Tables ... 26

Mixed 2 and 5 Times Tables 27

Mixed 2, 5 and
10 Times Tables 28

Repeated Addition 29

Puzzle: Maisie
and the Maze 30

Counting in 3s 32	Groups of 3 and 4 47
Groups of 3 33	Mixed 2 and 4 Times Tables 48
3 Times Table 34	Mixed 2 and 3 Times Tables 49
More 3 Times Table 35	Mixed 3 and 5 Times Tables 50
3 Times Table Facts 36	Mixed 4 and 10 Times Tables ... 51
More 3 Times Table Facts 37	Mixed 2, 3 and 5 Times Tables 52
Mixed 3 Times Table 38	Mixed 2, 4 and 10 Times Tables 53
Counting in 4s 39	
Groups of 4 40	Mixed 3, 4 and 5 Times Tables 54
4 Times Table 41	Mixed 3, 5 and 10 Times Tables 55
More 4 Times Table 42	
4 Times Table Facts 43	Mixed Times Tables 56
More 4 Times Table Facts 44	Word Problems 57
Mixed 4 Times Table 45	
Counting in 3s and 4s 46	Answers 58

Published by CGP

Editors: Molly Barker, Abigail Brindley, Liam Dyer, Sharon Keeley-Holden

With thanks to Sharon Gulliver and Glenn Rogers for the proofreading.

With thanks to Jan Greenway for the copyright research.

ISBN: 978 1 83774 023 9

Printed by Elanders Ltd, Newcastle upon Tyne.

Graphics used on the cover and throughout the book © Educlips 2023
Cover design concept by emc design ltd.

Text, design, layout and original illustrations
© Coordination Group Publications Ltd. (CGP) 2023
All rights reserved.

CGP, Broughton House, Griffin Street, Broughton-in-Furness, Cumbria, LA20 6HH

CGP c/o Elanders GmbH, Anton-Schmidt-Str. 15, 71332 Waiblingen, GERMANY. info@elanders-germany.com

Photocopying this book is not permitted, even if you have a CLA licence.
Extra copies are available from CGP with next day delivery • 0800 1712 712 • www.cgpbooks.co.uk

Counting in 2s

How It Works

Count in steps of two to fill in the missing numbers.

6   8   10   12

Now Try These

1. 2   ___   6   8   ___

2. ___   10   12   ___   16

3. ___   8   ___   12   14

4. 10   ___   14   16   ___

5. 12   14   ___   18   ___

6. 16   18   20   ___   ___

Awe-somersault! Grab a sticker.

Groups of 2

How It Works

Count the groups to fill in the missing number.

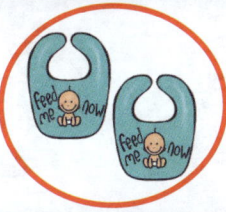 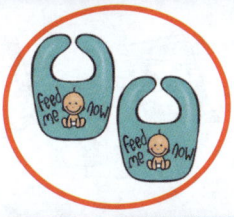 $\boxed{2} \times 2 = 4$

Now Try These

1. 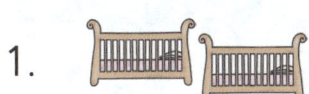   $\square \times 2 = 6$

2.     $\square \times 2 = 10$

3.        $\square \times 2 = 14$

4.    $\square \times 2 = 12$

5. 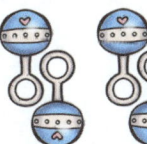       $\square \times 2 = 16$

6. 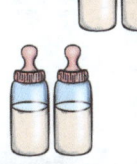  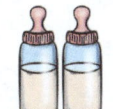 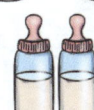 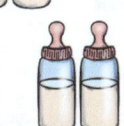  $\square \times 2 = 22$

You're doing great! Have a sticker.

2 Times Table

How It Works

Fill in the answer. Use the pictures to help you.

 $3 \times 2 =$ 6

Now Try These

1.

   $2 \times 2 =$ ☐

2.

   $4 \times 2 =$ ☐

3.

   $5 \times 2 =$ ☐

4.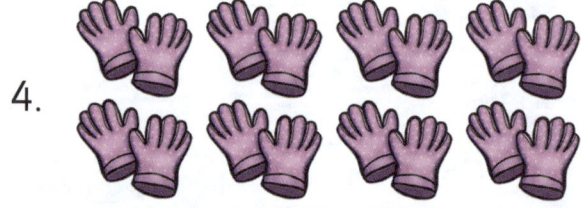

   $8 \times 2 =$ ☐

5.

   $6 \times 2 =$ ☐

6.

   $7 \times 2 =$ ☐

7.

   $10 \times 2 =$ ☐

8.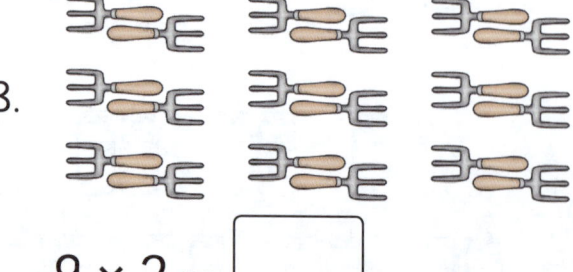

   $9 \times 2 =$ ☐

Fantastic! Plant a sticker here.

More 2 Times Table

How It Works

Draw lines to match each multiplication to its answer.

 8 × 2 — 16

Now Try These

1. 3 × 2
2. 5 × 2
3. 6 × 2
4. 9 × 2
5. 12 × 2
6. 4 × 2
7. 7 × 2

8
24
12
14
6
10
18

Hurray! Take a sticker.

2 Times Table Facts

How It Works

The crystals are shared into 2 equal groups. How many crystals are in each group?

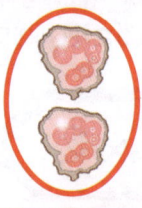 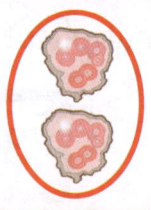 

2 in each group

Now Try These

1.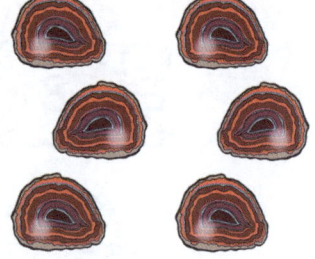

    ☐ in each group

4.

    ☐ in each group

2.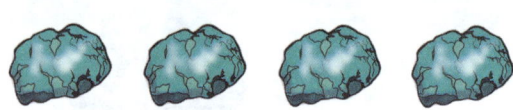

    ☐ in each group

5.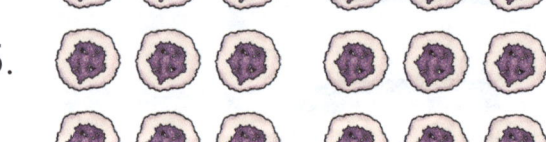

    ☐ in each group

3.

    ☐ in each group

6.

    ☐ in each group

Wow! Choose a sticker.

More 2 Times Table Facts

How It Works

Circle two equal groups. Use the groups to fill in the missing number.

6 ÷ 2 = 3

Now Try These

1.     2 ÷ 2 = ☐

2.     10 ÷ 2 = ☐

3.     16 ÷ 2 = ☐

4.     20 ÷ 2 = ☐

5. 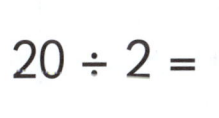   22 ÷ 2 = ☐

Bear-y good job! Swipe a sticker.

Mixed 2 Times Table

How It Works

Write the answer.
Use the pictures to help you.

$4 \times 2 =$ 8

Now Try These

1. $4 \div 2 =$ ☐

2. $3 \times 2 =$ ☐

3. $14 \div 2 =$ ☐

4. $6 \times 2 =$ ☐

5. $9 \times 2 =$ ☐

6. $22 \div 2 =$ ☐

7. $20 \div 2 =$ ☐

8. $12 \times 2 =$ ☐

Draw-some! Pick out a sticker.

Counting in 5s

How It Works

Fill in the missing numbers by counting in steps of five.

15 → 20 → **25**

Now Try These

1. 10 → ☐ → ☐

2. 0 → ☐ → ☐

3. 20 → 25 → ☐ → ☐

4. 15 → ☐ → 25 → ☐

5. 35 → ☐ → ☐ → 50

6. 45 → 50 → ☐ → ☐

Sm-art stuff! Treat yourself to a sticker.

Groups of 5

How It Works

Circle the correct answer.
Use the pictures to help you. 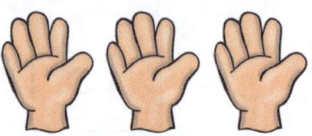 3 fives are 25 / ⓘ5

Now Try These

1. 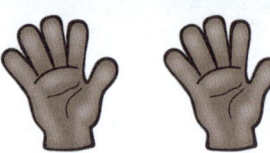 2 fives are 15 / 10

2. 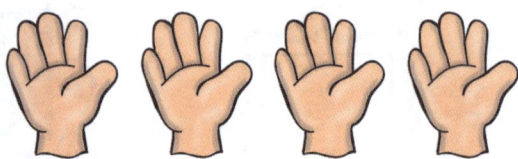 4 fives are 20 / 10

3.  5 fives are 25 / 30

4. 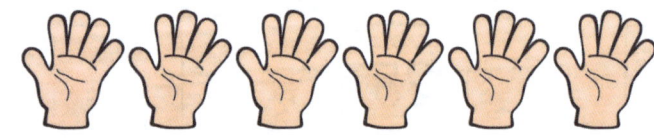 6 fives are 25 / 30

5.  8 fives are 40 / 30

6. 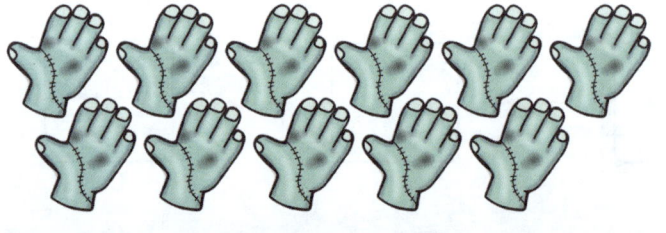 11 fives are 50 / 55

High five! Pop a sticker here.

5 Times Table

How It Works

Fill in the missing number. Use the pictures to help you.

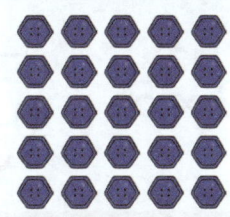 

Now Try These

1. ☐ × 5 = 10

2. ☐ × 5 = 15

3. ☐ × 5 = 20

4. ☐ × 5 = 30

5. ☐ × 5 = 35

6. ☐ × 5 = 45

Great job! Give yourself a sticker.

More 5 Times Table

How It Works

Circle the answer on the number line.

2 × 5

Now Try These

1. 1 × 5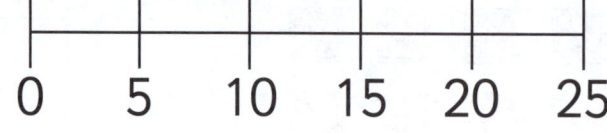

2. 3 × 5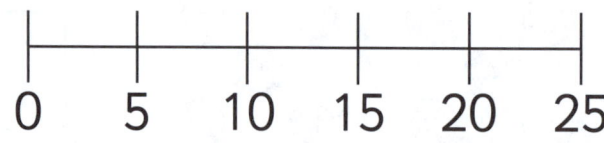

3. 4 × 5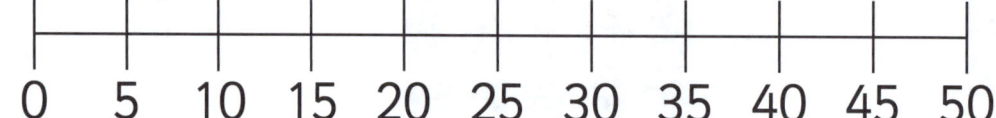

4. 7 × 5

5. 8 × 5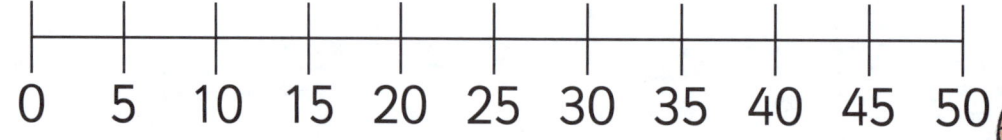

6. 10 × 5

Super! Choose a sticker.

5 Times Table Facts

How It Works

Circle 5 equal groups. Use the groups to fill in the missing numbers.

 15 ÷ 5 = 3

Now Try These

1.  10 ÷ 5 =

2.  25 ÷ 5 =

3.  30 ÷ 5 =

4.  45 ÷ 5 =

5. 55 ÷ 5 =

Sensation-owl! Place a sticker here.

More 5 Times Table Facts

How It Works

Circle the correct answer.

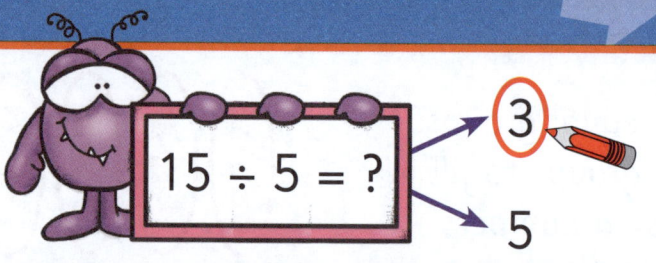

$15 \div 5 = ?$ → 3 / 5

Now Try These

1.  $10 \div 5 = ?$ → 3 / 2

5.  $35 \div 5 = ?$ → 6 / 7

2.  $20 \div 5 = ?$ → 4 / 5

6.  $40 \div 5 = ?$ → 8 / 6

3.  $30 \div 5 = ?$ → 8 / 6

7.  $45 \div 5 = ?$ → 10 / 9

4.  $25 \div 5 = ?$ → 5 / 7

8.  $55 \div 5 = ?$ → 11 / 12

Scary stuff! Have a sticker.

Mixed 5 Times Table

How It Works

Write × or ÷ to complete the number sentence.

2 × 5 = 10

Now Try These

1. 1 ☐ 5 = 5
2. 3 ☐ 5 = 15
3. 25 ☐ 5 = 5
4. 4 ☐ 5 = 20
5. 30 ☐ 5 = 6

6. 35 ☐ 5 = 7
7. 9 ☐ 5 = 45
8. 40 ☐ 5 = 8
9. 50 ☐ 5 = 10
10. 12 ☐ 5 = 60

Staying sharp! Pick up a sticker.

Counting in 10s

How It Works

Fill in the missing numbers by counting in steps of 10.

40   50   **60**

Now Try These

1. 10   ☐   30   40

2. 0   ☐   20   ☐

3. 30   ☐   ☐   60

4. 60   ☐   ☐   ☐

5. 80   90   ☐   ☐

You've earned your stripes! Get a sticker.

Groups of 10

How It Works

Count the snails to fill in the missing numbers. Each snail has 10 spots.

There are 2 snails,

so 2 × 10 = 20 spots.

Now Try These

1.

   There are ☐ snails, so ☐ × 10 = 30 spots.

2.

   There are ☐ snails, so ☐ × 10 = 50 spots.

3.

   There are ☐ snails, so ☐ × 10 = ☐ spots.

4.

   There are ☐ snails, so ☐ × 10 = ☐ spots.

5.

   There are ☐ snails, so ☐ × 10 = ☐ spots.

You s-nailed it! It's time for a sticker.

10 Times Table

How It Works

Write a multiplication shown by the pictures.

 4 × 10 = 40

Now Try These

1. ☐ × 10 = ☐

2. ☐ × 10 = ☐

3. ☐ × 10 = ☐

4. ☐ × 10 = ☐

5. ☐ × 10 = ☐

Sweet! Grab a sticker.

More 10 Times Table

How It Works

Tick the correct multiplication.

2 × 10 = 20

2 × 10 = 30 ☐

Now Try These

1. 1 × 10 = 10 ☐
    10 × 10 = 1 ☐

2. 3 × 10 = 3 ☐
    3 × 10 = 30 ☐

3. 50 = 5 × 10 ☐
    50 × 10 = 5 ☐

4. 70 = 6 × 10 ☐
    60 = 6 × 10 ☐

5. 70 × 10 = 7 ☐
    7 × 10 = 70 ☐

6. 8 × 10 = 80 ☐
    8 × 10 = 60 ☐

7. 90 × 10 = 9 ☐
    9 × 10 = 90 ☐

8. 100 × 10 = 10 ☐
    100 = 10 × 10 ☐

9. 110 = 11 × 10 ☐
    11 × 10 = 120 ☐

10. 12 × 10 = 100 ☐
    12 × 10 = 120 ☐

Well done! Choose a sticker.

10 Times Table Facts

How It Works

Fill in the missing numbers.

5 × 10 = 50, so 50 ÷ 10 = 5

Now Try These

1. 2 × 10 = 20, so ☐ ÷ 10 = ☐

2. 3 × 10 = 30, so ☐ ÷ 10 = ☐

3. 4 × 10 = 40, so ☐ ÷ 10 = ☐

4. 6 × 10 = 60, so ☐ ÷ 10 = ☐

5. 9 × 10 = 90, so ☐ ÷ 10 = ☐

6. 10 × 10 = 100, so ☐ ÷ 10 = ☐

7. 11 × 10 = 110, so ☐ ÷ 10 = ☐

Snow way! Put a sticker here.

More 10 Times Table Facts

How It Works

Fill in the missing answer.   10 ÷ 10 = 1

Now Try These

1. 30 ÷ 10 =
2. 50 ÷ 10 =
3. 40 ÷ 10 =
4. 60 ÷ 10 =
5. 70 ÷ 10 =

6. 90 ÷ 10 =
7. 80 ÷ 10 =
8. 100 ÷ 10 =
9. 110 ÷ 10 =
10. 120 ÷ 10 =

Mer-mazing! You deserve a sticker.

Mixed 10 Times Table

How It Works

Draw lines to match each calculation to its answer.

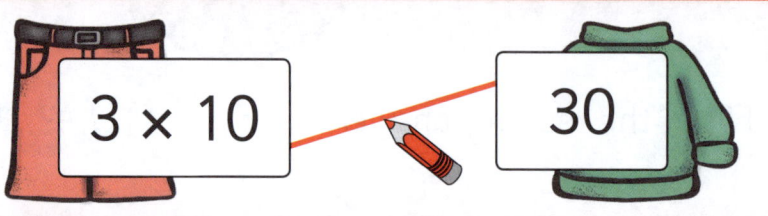

Now Try These

1.  9×10

2. 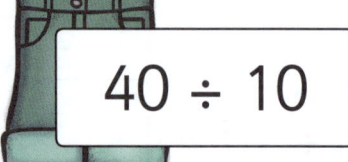 $40 \div 10$  90

3.  6×10  10

4.  $70 \div 10$  4

5.  $100 \div 10$  110

6.  11×10  7

                                        60

Fantastic! Pick out a sticker.

Counting in 2s, 5s and 10s

How It Works

Count in steps to find the missing numbers.

Now Try These

1.
   15, 20, 25, __, __

2.
   40, 50, 60, __, __

3.
   16, 18, 20, __, __

4.
   40, __, 50, __, 60

5.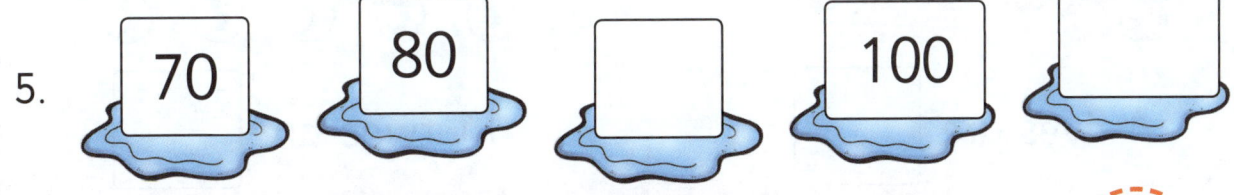
   70, 80, __, 100, __

You're making a splash! Place a sticker here.

Groups of 2, 5 and 10

How It Works

Fill in the missing number. Use the pictures to help you.

 3 fives are 15

Now Try These

1. 4 twos are ☐

2. 2 tens are ☐

3. 4 fives are ☐

4. 6 tens are ☐

5. 8 fives are ☐

6. 11 twos are ☐

Great effort! Have a sticker.

24

Mixed 2 and 10 Times Tables

How It Works

Circle the mugs with a number in the times table shown.

Now Try These

1.

4.

2.

5.

3.

6.

You're doing great! Choose a sticker.

Mixed 5 and 10 Times Tables

How It Works

Write × or ÷ to complete the number sentence.

4 × 5 = 20

Now Try These

1. 3 ☐ 10 = 30

2. 40 ☐ 10 = 4

3. 35 ☐ 5 = 7

4. 5 ☐ 10 = 50

5. 25 ☐ 5 = 5

6. 9 = 45 ☐ 5

7. 60 = 12 ☐ 5

8. 8 ☐ 10 = 80

9. 11 = 55 ☐ 5

10. 11 ☐ 10 = 110

Meow-vellous! Snag yourself a sticker.

Mixed 2 and 5 Times Tables

How It Works

Fill in the answer.   18 ÷ 2 = 9

Now Try These

1. 5 × 2 =

2. 12 ÷ 2 =

3. 15 ÷ 5 =

4. 6 × 5 =

5. 6 × 2 =

6. 14 ÷ 2 =

7. 40 ÷ 5 =

8. 10 × 5 =

9. 11 × 2 =

10. 60 ÷ 5 =

Wow! You've earned a sticker.

Mixed 2, 5 and 10 Times Tables

How It Works

Fill in the missing number.   2 × 4 = 8

Now Try These

1. 2 × 5 = ☐
2. ☐ ÷ 10 = 2
3. ☐ ÷ 2 = 3
4. 8 × 5 = ☐
5. ☐ ÷ 5 = 5

6. ☐ × 2 = 16
7. 50 ÷ 10 = ☐
8. ☐ × 5 = 45
9. 24 ÷ 2 = ☐
10. ☐ × 10 = 120

Fabulous! Goat and get a sticker.

Repeated Addition

How It Works

Put a cross in the box next to the calculation that gives a different answer.

☐ 10 + 10 + 10 + 10
☐ 4 × 10
✗ 4 + 4 + 4 + 4

Now Try These

1. ☐ 3 × 2
   ☐ 2 × 2
   ☐ 2 + 2 + 2

2. ☐ 2 + 2
   ☐ 2 × 10
   ☐ 10 × 2

3. ☐ 10 + 10 + 10
   ☐ 3 + 3 + 3
   ☐ 3 × 10

4. ☐ 4 × 2
   ☐ 2 + 2 + 2 + 2
   ☐ 4 + 4 + 4

5. ☐ 4 × 5
   ☐ 5 × 5
   ☐ 5 + 5 + 5 + 5 + 5

6. ☐ 6 × 10
   ☐ 6 + 6 + 6 + 6 + 6 + 6
   ☐ 10 × 6

7. ☐ 7 × 5
   ☐ 5 × 7
   ☐ 5 + 5 + 5 + 5 + 5

8. ☐ 5 + 5 + 5 + 5 + 5 + 5
   ☐ 5 × 5
   ☐ 6 × 5

Wonderful! Pick out a sticker.

Maisie and the Maze

Maisie and her friends are lost in a maze. Use your stickers to solve problems and help them escape!

1 Put a sticker next to every number in the 5 times table.

Start

25
18
15
51
12
10

10 ÷ 10 = 100
7 × 5 = 35
20 ÷ 2 = 10
7 × 2 = 14
24 ÷ 4 = 6
8 × 5 = 45

2 Add some crocodile stickers. Fill in the missing numbers to cross the bridges.

9 × ☐ = 18

30

Take this compass!

Parachute down when you're done!

3 × 4

4 Colour in pairs of calculations with the same answer. Use a different colour for each pair.

3 × 2

3 × 10

2 × 3

6 × 2

6 × 5

Avoid the yeti!

Exit

Pick up a map!

There's treasure ahead! Add stickers of the friends you've seen to help you dig.

3 Tick all the correct calculations you see.

Collect the treasure!

☐ ÷ 10 = 11

5 Fill in the missing numbers below using the pictures.

There are...

☐ × ☐ = 40 coins.

31

Counting in 3s

How It Works

Count in steps of three to fill in the missing numbers.

Now Try These

1.

2.

3.

4.

5.

6.

Awesome! Give yourself a sticker.

Groups of 3

How It Works

Count the groups to fill in the missing numbers.

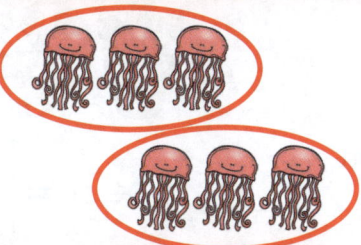

2 × 3 = 6

Now Try These

1.   ☐ × 3 = ☐

2.  ☐ × 3 = ☐

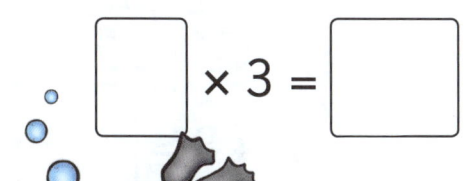

3. 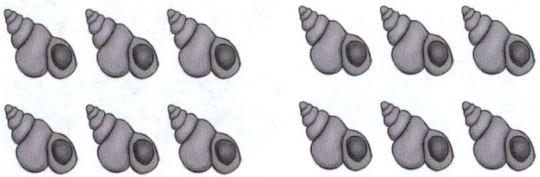 ☐ × 3 = ☐

4.  ☐ × 3 = ☐

5. ☐ × 3 = ☐

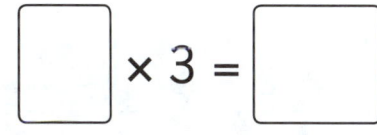

You're a star! Have a sticker.

3 Times Table

How It Works

Fill in the answer.
Use the pictures to help you.

3 × 3 = 9

Now Try These

1.

    1 × 3 =

2.

    2 × 3 =

3.

    6 × 3 =

4.

    7 × 3 =

5.

    5 × 3 =

6.

    4 × 3 =

7.

    8 × 3 =

8.

    10 × 3 =

Lovely! Take a sticker.

More 3 Times Table

How It Works

Circle the answer on the number line.

2 × 3

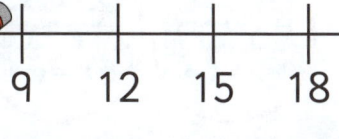

Now Try These

1. 4 × 3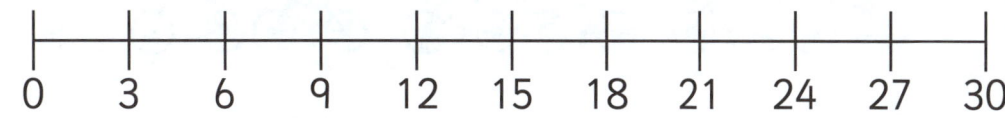

2. 3 × 3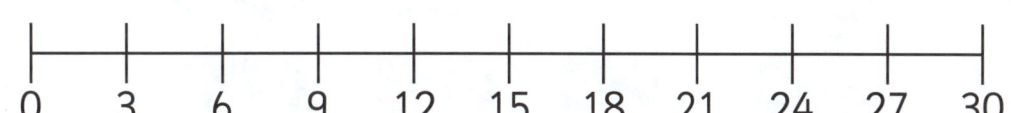

3. 7 × 3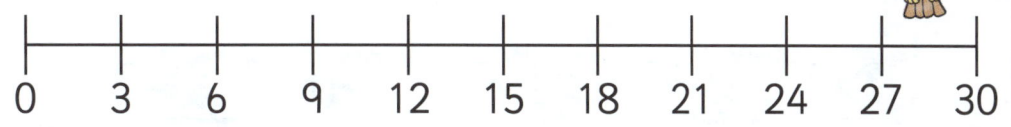

4. 5 × 3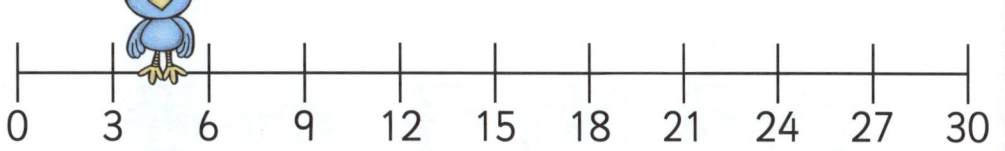

5. 9 × 3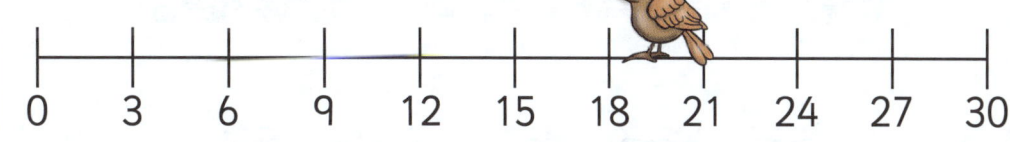

6. 8 × 3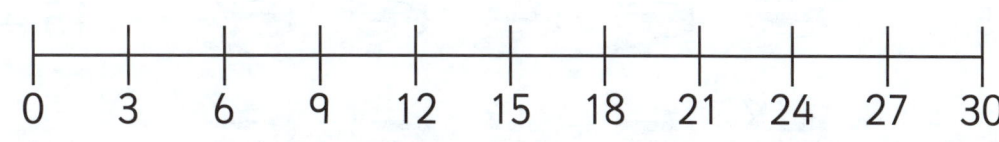

Marvellous! Choose a sticker.

3 Times Table Facts

How It Works

Circle 3 equal groups. Use the groups to fill in the answer.

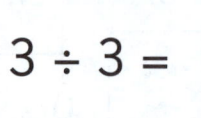   3 ÷ 3 = 1

Now Try These

1. 6 ÷ 3 =

2. 12 ÷ 3 =

3. 9 ÷ 3 =

4. 18 ÷ 3 =

5. 15 ÷ 3 =

That was great work! Grab a sticker.

36

More 3 Times Table Facts

How It Works

Fill in the missing number in the division.

6 ÷ 3 = 2

Now Try These

1. 9 ÷ 3 = ☐
2. 15 ÷ 3 = ☐
3. ☐ ÷ 3 = 4
4. 18 ÷ 3 = ☐
5. ☐ ÷ 3 = 8

6. ☐ ÷ 3 = 7
7. 30 ÷ 3 = ☐
8. ☐ ÷ 3 = 9
9. 36 ÷ 3 = ☐
10. 33 ÷ 3 = ☐

Super! Put a sticker here.

Mixed 3 Times Table

How It Works

Make two different number sentences using numbers from the box.

3   15   5

5 × 3 = 15

3 × 5 = 15

Now Try These

1. 12   3   4

☐ × ☐ = ☐
☐ × ☐ = ☐

2. 24   3   8

☐ ÷ ☐ = ☐
☐ ÷ ☐ = ☐

3. 7   21   3

☐ × ☐ = ☐
☐ × ☐ = ☐

4. 3   33   11

☐ ÷ ☐ = ☐
☐ ÷ ☐ = ☐

5. 9   27   3

☐ × ☐ = ☐
☐ × ☐ = ☐

6. 3   36   12

☐ ÷ ☐ = ☐
☐ ÷ ☐ = ☐

Amazing! Have a sticker.

Counting in 4s

How It Works

Count in steps of four to fill in the missing numbers.

4   8   12

Now Try These

1. 8   12   ☐   20   ☐

2. 16   ☐   24   28   ☐

3. ☐   ☐   12   16   20

4. 32   36   ☐   44   ☐

5. ☐   32   ☐   40   ☐

Brilliant! Find a sticker.

Groups of 4

How It Works

How many blocks altogether?

 2 fours are [8], so 2 × 4 = [8]

Now Try These

1.  1 four is [   ], so 1 × 4 = [   ]

2.  5 fours are [   ], so 5 × 4 = [   ]

3.  3 fours are [   ], so 3 × 4 = [   ]

4.  4 fours are [   ], so 4 × 4 = [   ]

5.  6 fours are [   ], so 6 × 4 = [   ]

Great job! Pick a sticker.

40

4 Times Table

How It Works

Write the answer.
Use the pictures to help you.

     3 × 4 = 12

Now Try These

1.

    2 × 4 = ☐

2.

    4 × 4 = ☐

3.

    7 × 4 = ☐

4.

    6 × 4 = ☐

5.

    5 × 4 = ☐

6.

    9 × 4 = ☐

7.

    8 × 4 = ☐

8.

    10 × 4 = ☐

Spot on! Choose a sticker.

More 4 Times Table

How It Works

Draw lines to match each calculation to its answer.

Now Try These

1. 3×4
2. 9×4
3. 12×4
4. 4×8
5. 5×4
6. 4×6
7. 11×4

Paw-some! Take a sticker.

4 Times Table Facts

How It Works

Share the acorns equally between 4 squirrels. How many acorns does each squirrel get?

 **2** acorns

Now Try These

1.    ☐ acorn

2.      ☐ acorns

3.  ☐ acorns

4.      ☐ acorns

5.       ☐ acorns

6.    ☐ acorns

Great work! Give yourself a sticker.

More 4 Times Table Facts

How It Works

Fill in the missing number in the division.

12 ÷ 4 = 3

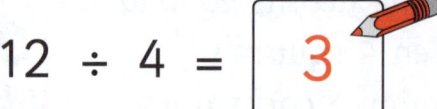

Now Try These

1. 8 ÷ 4 = ☐
2. 16 ÷ 4 = ☐
3. 24 ÷ 4 = ☐
4. 28 ÷ 4 = ☐
5. ☐ ÷ 4 = 5

6. 40 ÷ 4 = ☐
7. ☐ ÷ 4 = 9
8. 32 ÷ 4 = ☐
9. ☐ ÷ 4 = 12
10. 44 ÷ 4 = ☐

Wonderful! Pick a sticker.

Mixed 4 Times Table

How It Works

Tick the correct calculation.

$4 \div 4 = 2$ ☐

$8 \div 4 = 2$ ☑

Now Try These

1. $2 \times 4 = 8$ ☐
   $5 \times 4 = 8$ ☐

2. $16 \div 4 = 4$ ☐
   $20 \div 4 = 4$ ☐

3. $4 \times 4 = 12$ ☐
   $3 \times 4 = 12$ ☐

4. $28 \div 4 = 8$ ☐
   $28 \div 4 = 7$ ☐

5. $6 \times 4 = 24$ ☐
   $6 \times 4 = 20$ ☐

6. $32 \div 4 = 6$ ☐
   $32 \div 4 = 8$ ☐

7. $10 \times 4 = 40$ ☐
   $11 \times 4 = 40$ ☐

8. $36 \div 4 = 8$ ☐
   $36 \div 4 = 9$ ☐

9. $8 \times 4 = 48$ ☐
   $12 \times 4 = 48$ ☐

10. $44 \div 4 = 11$ ☐
    $44 \div 4 = 10$ ☐

Great job! Place a sticker here.

Counting in 3s and 4s

How It Works

Count in steps to fill in the missing numbers.

3 → 6 → 9 → 12

Now Try These

1. 4 → ☐ → 12 → 16 → ☐

2. 9 → 12 → ☐ → ☐ → 21

3. 20 → ☐ → 28 → ☐ → 36

4. ☐ → 27 → ☐ → 33 → 36

5. ☐ → ☐ → 20 → 24 → ☐

6. 32 → ☐ → ☐ → 44 → ☐

Score! Grab a sticker.

46

Groups of 3 and 4

How It Works

Fill in the answer.
Use the pictures to help you.

3 fours are 12

Now Try These

1.

   3 threes are ☐

2.

   5 fours are ☐

3.

   6 threes are ☐

4.

   4 fours are ☐

5.

   8 threes are ☐

6.

   6 fours are ☐

7.

   7 threes are ☐

8.

   8 fours are ☐

Party time! Take a sticker.

Mixed 2 and 4 Times Tables

How It Works

Fill in the answer. $3 \times 2 = \boxed{6}$

Now Try These

1. $5 \times 2 = \boxed{}$
2. $2 \times 4 = \boxed{}$
3. $4 \times 4 = \boxed{}$
4. $7 \times 2 = \boxed{}$
5. $8 \times 4 = \boxed{}$

6. $8 \times 2 = \boxed{}$
7. $11 \times 2 = \boxed{}$
8. $9 \times 4 = \boxed{}$
9. $10 \times 2 = \boxed{}$
10. $12 \times 4 = \boxed{}$

Brrr-illiant! Put a sticker here.

Mixed 2 and 3 Times Tables

How It Works

Tick the box to show which times table the number is in.

- [ ] 2 times table
- [✓] 3 times table
- [ ] Both

Now Try These

1.
   - [ ] 2 times table
   - [ ] 3 times table
   - [ ] Both

5.
   - [ ] 2 times table
   - [ ] 3 times table
   - [ ] Both

2.
   - [ ] 2 times table
   - [ ] 3 times table
   - [ ] Both

6.
   - [ ] 2 times table
   - [ ] 3 times table
   - [ ] Both

3.
   - [ ] 2 times table
   - [ ] 3 times table
   - [ ] Both

7.
   - [ ] 2 times table
   - [ ] 3 times table
   - [ ] Both

4.
   - [ ] 2 times table
   - [ ] 3 times table
   - [ ] Both

8.
   - [ ] 2 times table
   - [ ] 3 times table
   - [ ] Both

Spook-tacular! Choose a sticker.

Mixed 3 and 5 Times Tables

How It Works

Fill in the missing number.   4 × [3] = 12

Now Try These

1. 9 × 3 = ☐

2. 50 ÷ 5 = ☐

3. 3 × 5 = ☐

4. 40 ÷ 5 = ☐

5. 8 × ☐ = 24

6. 5 × ☐ = 25

7. ☐ ÷ 3 = 12

8. 11 × 5 = ☐

9. 12 ÷ ☐ = 4

10. ☐ × 5 = 35

Brilliant! Place a sticker here.

Mixed 4 and 10 Times Tables

How It Works

Fill in the boxes to find the total cost of the items.

Golden Eggs — 10p each

Magic Beans — 4p each

2 golden eggs

2 × 10 p = 20 p

Now Try These

1. 3 magic beans   3 × ☐ p = ☐ p

2. 5 golden eggs   5 × ☐ p = ☐ p

3. 10 magic beans   10 × ☐ p = ☐ p

4. 12 golden eggs   12 × ☐ p = ☐ p

5. 9 golden eggs   9 × ☐ p = ☐ p

6. 7 magic beans   7 × ☐ p = ☐ p

7. 11 magic beans   11 × ☐ p = ☐ p

Magical! Give yourself a sticker.

Mixed 2, 3 and 5 Times Tables

How It Works

Circle the calculation that gives the answer in the box.

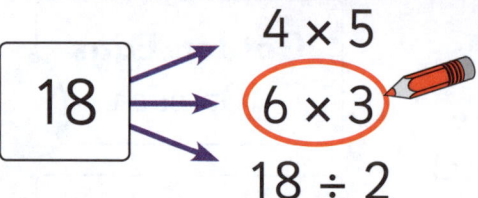

Now Try These

1. 8 → 2 × 5 / 8 ÷ 2 / 4 × 2

2. 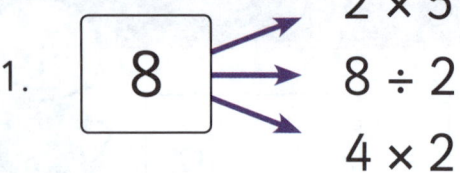 4 → 12 ÷ 3 / 1 × 5 / 16 ÷ 2

3. 30 → 8 × 3 / 25 ÷ 5 / 6 × 5

4. 22 → 20 ÷ 2 / 11 × 2 / 4 × 5

5. 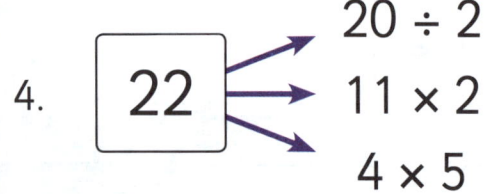 35 → 6 × 5 / 7 × 5 / 36 ÷ 3

6. 12 → 60 ÷ 5 / 6 × 3 / 24 ÷ 3

7. 11 → 36 ÷ 3 / 11 × 2 / 22 ÷ 2

8. 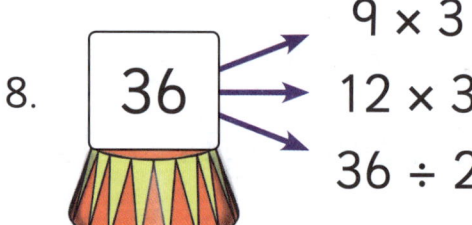 36 → 9 × 3 / 12 × 3 / 36 ÷ 2

9. 9 → 27 ÷ 3 / 3 × 5 / 24 ÷ 2

10. 6 → 14 ÷ 2 / 12 ÷ 3 / 30 ÷ 5

Top stuff! Pick out a sticker.

Mixed 2, 4 and 10 Times Tables

How It Works

Fill in the missing numbers in the pair of calculations.

$16 \div \boxed{2} = 8$

$8 \times 2 = \boxed{16}$

Now Try These

1. $32 \div \boxed{} = 8$

   $8 \times 4 = \boxed{}$

2. $20 \div \boxed{} = 10$

   $\boxed{} \times 2 = 20$

3. $7 \times 4 = \boxed{}$

   $28 \div \boxed{} = 7$

4. $40 \div \boxed{} = 10$

   $4 \times \boxed{} = 40$

5. $44 \div \boxed{} = 11$

   $4 \times 11 = \boxed{}$

6. $24 \div 6 = \boxed{}$

   $6 \times \boxed{} = 24$

You're amazing! Find a sticker.

Mixed 3, 4 and 5 Times Tables

How It Works

Write a correct number sentence using the numbers and symbol.

×, 9, 3

9 × 3 = 27

Now Try These

40, 8, ÷

1. ☐ = 5

3, 18, ÷

6. ☐ = 6

×, 9, 4

2. ☐ = 36

4, ÷, 16

7. 4 = ☐

3, ÷, 30

3. ☐ = 10

5, 9, ×

8. 45 = ☐

×, 5, 3

4. ☐ = 15

×, 3, 8

9. ☐ = 24

11, 4, ×

5. ☐ = 44

6, 30, ÷

10. 5 = ☐

Fantas-tech! Choose a sticker.

Mixed 3, 5 and 10 Times Tables

How It Works

Circle the calculation that is wrong.

| $30 ÷ 3 = 10$ | $(6 × 5 = 3)$ | $30 ÷ 5 = 6$ |

Now Try These

1. $18 ÷ 3 = 6$ $3 × 5 = 20$

2. $6 × 5 = 30$ $30 ÷ 10 = 5$

3. $9 × 10 = 90$ $5 ÷ 50 = 10$ $4 × 5 = 20$

4. $12 × 3 = 36$ $18 ÷ 3 = 6$ $20 ÷ 5 = 2$

5. $9 × 3 = 27$ $9 × 5 = 35$ $10 ÷ 5 = 2$

6. $55 ÷ 11 = 5$ $30 ÷ 3 = 9$ $5 × 7 = 35$

What a workout! Take a sticker.

Mixed Times Tables

How It Works

Draw lines to match calculations that give the same answer.

2 × 3 — 12 ÷ 2

Now Try These

1. 1 × 5   5 × 4
2. 12 ÷ 2   6 ÷ 3
3. 2 × 10   30 ÷ 6
4. 2 × 5   6 × 4
5. 24 ÷ 2   4 × 3
6. 2 × 12   100 ÷ 10
7. 4 × 4   18 ÷ 3
8. 16 ÷ 8   8 × 2

Hooray! Have a sticker.

Word Problems

How It Works

3 roses and 4 tulips grow from 1 packet of seeds. How many flowers grow from more packets?

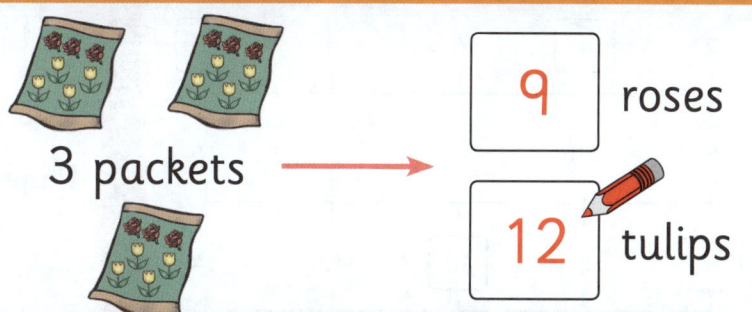

3 packets → 9 roses
12 tulips

Now Try These

1. 2 packets → ☐ roses ☐ tulips
2. 4 packets → ☐ roses ☐ tulips
3. 10 packets → ☐ roses ☐ tulips
4. 5 packets → ☐ roses ☐ tulips
5. 8 packets → ☐ roses ☐ tulips
6. 9 packets → ☐ roses ☐ tulips
7. 12 packets → ☐ roses ☐ tulips

Well done! Put a sticker here.

Answers

Page 2 — Counting in 2s

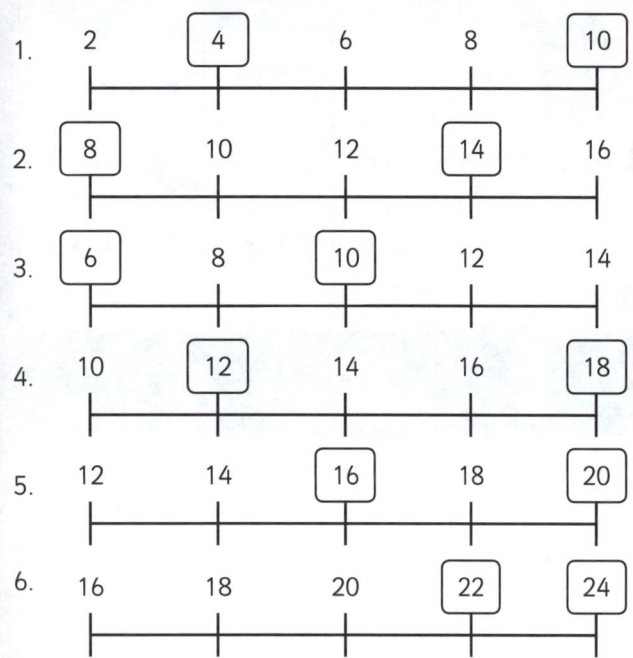

Page 3 — Groups of 2

1. 3
2. 5
3. 7
4. 6
5. 8
6. 11

Page 4 — 2 Times Table

1. 4
2. 8
3. 10
4. 16
5. 12
6. 14
7. 20
8. 18

Page 5 — More 2 Times Table

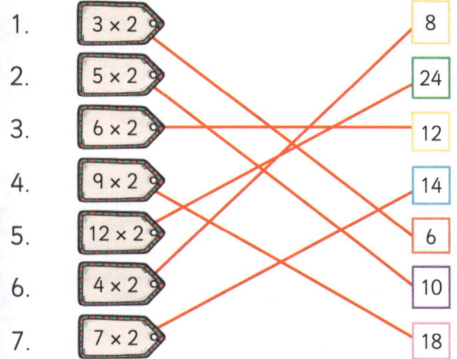

Page 6 — 2 Times Table Facts

1. 3
2. 4
3. 6
4. 7
5. 9
6. 11

Page 7 — More 2 Times Table Facts

1. 1
2. 5
3. 8
4. 10
5. 11

Page 8 — Mixed 2 Times Table

1. 2
2. 6
3. 7
4. 12
5. 18
6. 11
7. 10
8. 24

Page 9 — Counting in 5s

1. 10 → **15** → **20**
2. 0 → **5** → **10**
3. 20 → 25 → **30** → **35**
4. 15 → **20** → 25 → **30**
5. 35 → **40** → **45** → 50
6. 45 → 50 → **55** → **60**

Page 10 — Groups of 5

1. 2 fives are **10**
2. 4 fives are **20**
3. 5 fives are **25**
4. 6 fives are **30**
5. 8 fives are **40**
6. 11 fives are **55**

Page 11 — 5 Times Table

1. 2
2. 3
3. 4
4. 6
5. 7
6. 9

Page 12 — More 5 Times Table

1. 5
2. 15
3. 20
4. 35
5. 40
6. 50

Answers

Page 13 — 5 Times Table Facts
1. 2
2. 5
3. 6
4. 9
5. 11

Page 14 — More 5 Times Table Facts
1. 2
2. 4
3. 6
4. 5
5. 7
6. 8
7. 9
8. 11

Page 15 — Mixed 5 Times Table
1. 1 × 5 = **5**
2. 3 × 5 = **15**
3. 25 ÷ 5 = **5**
4. 4 × 5 = **20**
5. 30 ÷ 5 = **6**
6. 35 ÷ 5 = **7**
7. 9 × 5 = **45**
8. 40 ÷ 5 = **8**
9. 50 ÷ 5 = **10**
10. 12 × 5 = **60**

Page 16 — Counting in 10s

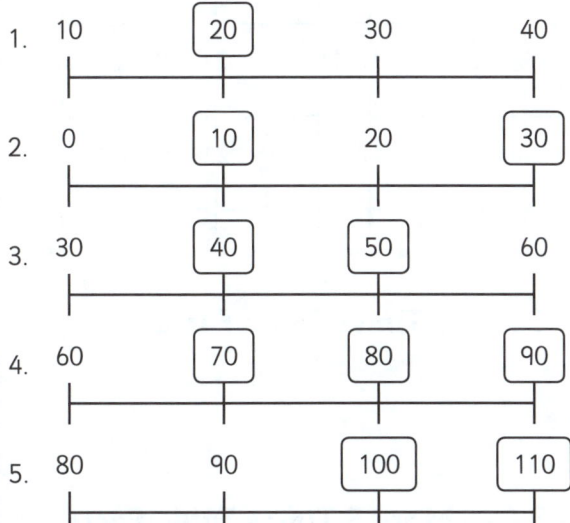

Page 17 — Groups of 10
1. There are **3** snails, so **3** × 10 = **30** spots.
2. There are **5** snails, so **5** × 10 = **50** spots.
3. There are **4** snails, so **4** × 10 = **40** spots.
4. There are **8** snails, so **8** × 10 = **80** spots.
5. There are **7** snails, so **7** × 10 = **70** spots.

Page 18 — 10 Times Table
1. **2** × 10 = **20**
2. **3** × 10 = **30**
3. **5** × 10 = **50**
4. **6** × 10 = **60**
5. **8** × 10 = **80**

Page 19 — More 10 Times Table
1. 1 × 10 = 10
2. 3 × 10 = 30
3. 50 = 5 × 10
4. 60 = 6 × 10
5. 7 × 10 = 70
6. 8 × 10 = 80
7. 9 × 10 = 90
8. 100 = 10 × 10
9. 110 = 11 × 10
10. 12 × 10 = 120

Page 20 — 10 Times Table Facts
1. 2 × 10 = 20, so **20** ÷ 10 = **2**
2. 3 × 10 = 30, so **30** ÷ 10 = **3**
3. 4 × 10 = 40, so **40** ÷ 10 = **4**
4. 6 × 10 = 60, so **60** ÷ 10 = **6**
5. 9 × 10 = 90, so **90** ÷ 10 = **9**
6. 10 × 10 = 100, so **100** ÷ 10 = **10**
7. 11 × 10 = 110, so **110** ÷ 10 = **11**

Page 21 — More 10 Times Table Facts
1. 3
2. 5
3. 4
4. 6
5. 7
6. 9
7. 8
8. 10
9. 11
10. 12

Page 22 — Mixed 10 Times Table

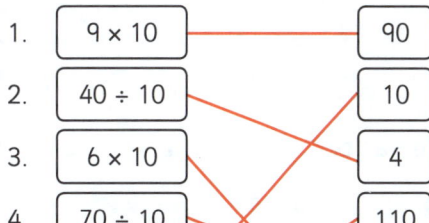

Page 23 — Counting in 2s, 5s and 10s
1. 15, 20, 25, **30**, 35
2. 40, 50, 60, **70**, **80**
3. 16, 18, 20, **22**, **24**
4. 40, **45**, 50, **55**, 60
5. 70, 80, **90**, 100, **110**

Page 24 — Groups of 2, 5 and 10
1. 8
2. 20
3. 20
4. 60
5. 40
6. 22

Answers

Page 25 — Mixed 2 and 10 Times Tables
1. ⓣ30 15 ⓣ20   4. 17 ⓣ18 19
2. 11 ⓣ10 12   5. ⓣ40 45 ⓣ50 48
3. ⓣ12 ⓣ8 9   6. 15 ⓣ16 ⓣ18 21

Page 26 — Mixed 5 and 10 Times Tables
1. ×   6. ÷
2. ÷   7. ×
3. ÷   8. ×
4. ×   9. ÷
5. ÷   10. ×

Page 27 — Mixed 2 and 5 Times Tables
1. 10   6. 7
2. 6   7. 8
3. 3   8. 50
4. 30   9. 22
5. 12   10. 12

Page 28 — Mixed 2, 5 and 10 Times Tables
1. 10   6. 8
2. 20   7. 5
3. 6   8. 9
4. 40   9. 12
5. 25   10. 12

Page 29 — Repeated Addition
1. 2 × 2   5. 4 × 5
2. 2 + 2   6. 6 + 6 + 6 + 6 + 6 + 6
3. 3 + 3 + 3   7. 5 + 5 + 5 + 5 + 5
4. 4 + 4 + 4 + 4   8. 5 × 5

Pages 30-31 — Maisie and the Maze
1. 25, 15, 10
2. 9 × **2** = 18
   110 ÷ 10 = 11
3. 20 ÷ 2 = 10
   7 × 2 = 14
   24 ÷ 4 = 6
   7 × 5 = 35
4. 3 × 4 | 6 × 2
   2 × 3 | 3 × 2
   6 × 5 | 3 × 10
5. **4 × 10** = 40 coins
   or **10 × 4** = 40 coins.

Page 32 — Counting in 3s
1. 3, 6, 9, **12**, **15**   4. 18, 21, **24**, 27, **30**
2. 0, **3**, 6, **9**, 12   5. **3**, **6**, 9, 12, 15
3. 12, 15, **18**, **21**, 24   6. 24, **27**, 30, **33**, 36

Page 33 — Groups of 3
1. **1** × 3 = **3**   4. **5** × 3 = **15**
2. **3** × 3 = **9**   5. **6** × 3 = **18**
3. **4** × 3 = **12**

Page 34 — 3 Times Table
1. 3   5. 15
2. 6   6. 12
3. 18   7. 24
4. 21   8. 30

Page 35 — More 3 Times Table
1. 12 circled on number line
2. 9 circled
3. 21 circled
4. 15 circled
5. 27 circled
6. 24 circled

Page 36 — 3 Times Table Facts
1. 2   4. 6
2. 4   5. 5
3. 3

Page 37 — More 3 Times Table Facts
1. 3   6. 21
2. 5   7. 10
3. 12   8. 27
4. 6   9. 12
5. 24   10. 11

Page 38 — Mixed 3 Times Table
1. 4 × 3 = 12   4. 33 ÷ 3 = 11
   3 × 4 = 12   33 ÷ 11 = 3
2. 24 ÷ 3 = 8   5. 9 × 3 = 27
   24 ÷ 8 = 3   3 × 9 = 27
3. 7 × 3 = 21   6. 36 ÷ 3 = 12
   3 × 7 = 21   36 ÷ 12 = 3

Answers

Page 39 — Counting in 4s

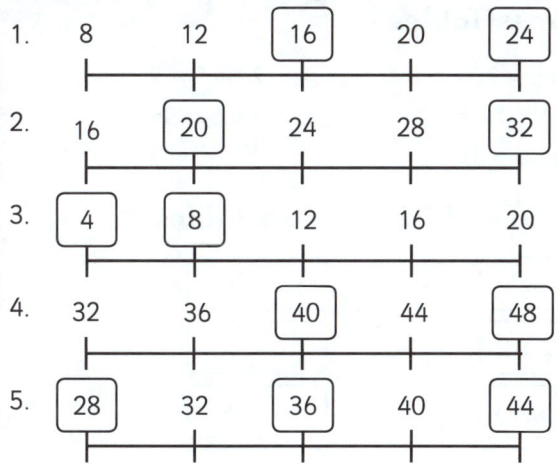

Page 40 — Groups of 4

1. 1 four is **4**, so 1 × 4 = **4**
2. 5 fours are **20**, so 5 × 4 = **20**
3. 3 fours are **12**, so 3 × 4 = **12**
4. 4 fours are **16**, so 4 × 4 = **16**
5. 6 fours are **24**, so 6 × 4 = **24**

Page 41 — 4 Times Table

1. 8
2. 16
3. 28
4. 24
5. 20
6. 36
7. 32
8. 40

Page 42 — More 4 Times Table

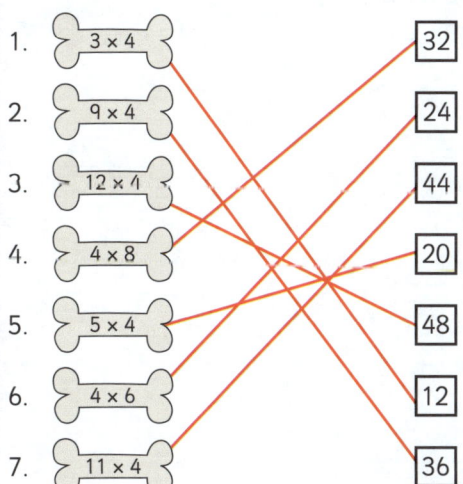

Page 43 — 4 Times Table Facts

1. 1 acorn
2. 4 acorns
3. 5 acorns
4. 3 acorns
5. 2 acorns
6. 6 acorns

Page 44 — More 4 Times Table Facts

1. 2
2. 4
3. 6
4. 7
5. 20
6. 10
7. 36
8. 8
9. 48
10. 11

Page 45 — Mixed 4 Times Table

1. 2 × 4 = 8
2. 16 ÷ 4 = 4
3. 3 × 4 = 12
4. 28 ÷ 4 = 7
5. 6 × 4 = 24
6. 32 ÷ 4 = 8
7. 10 × 4 = 40
8. 36 ÷ 4 = 9
9. 12 × 4 = 48
10. 44 ÷ 4 = 11

Page 46 — Counting in 3s and 4s

1. 4, 8, 12, 16, 20
2. 9, 12, 15, 18, 21
3. 20, 24, 28, 32, 36
4. 24, 27, 30, 33, 36
5. 12, 16, 20, 24, 28
6. 32, 36, 40, 44, 48

Page 47 — Groups of 3 and 4

1. 9
2. 20
3. 18
4. 16
5. 24
6. 24
7. 21
8. 32

Page 48 — Mixed 2 and 4 Times Tables

1. 10
2. 8
3. 16
4. 14
5. 32
6. 16
7. 22
8. 36
9. 20
10. 48

Page 49 — Mixed 2 and 3 Times Tables

1. 2 times table
2. Both
3. 3 times table
4. Both
5. 2 times table
6. 3 times table
7. Both
8. 3 times table

Answers

Page 50 — Mixed 3 and 5 Times Tables
1. 9 × 3 = **27**
2. 50 ÷ 5 = **10**
3. 3 × 5 = **15**
4. 40 ÷ 5 = **8**
5. 8 × **3** = 24
6. 5 × **5** = 25
7. **36** ÷ 3 = 12
8. 11 × 5 = **55**
9. 12 ÷ **3** = 4
10. **7** × 5 = 35

Page 51 — Mixed 4 and 10 Times Tables
1. 3 × **4**p = **12**p
2. 5 × **10**p = **50**p
3. 10 × **4**p = **40**p
4. 12 × **10**p = **120**p
5. 9 × **10**p = **90**p
6. 7 × **4**p = **28**p
7. 11 × **4**p = **44**p

Page 52 — Mixed 2, 3 and 5 Times Tables
1. 4 × 2
2. 12 ÷ 3
3. 6 × 5
4. 11 × 2
5. 7 × 5
6. 60 ÷ 5
7. 22 ÷ 2
8. 12 × 3
9. 27 ÷ 3
10. 30 ÷ 5

Page 53 — Mixed 2, 4 and 10 Times Tables
1. 32 ÷ **4** = 8
   8 × 4 = **32**
2. 20 ÷ **2** = 10
   10 × 2 = 20
3. 7 × 4 = **28**
   28 ÷ **4** = 7
4. 40 ÷ **4** = 10
   4 × **10** = 40
5. 44 ÷ **4** = 11
   4 × 11 = **44**
6. 24 ÷ 6 = **4**
   6 × **4** = 24

Page 54 — Mixed 3, 4 and 5 Times Tables
1. **40** ÷ **8** = 5
2. **9** × **4** = 36 or **4** × **9** = 36
3. **30** ÷ **3** = 10
4. **3** × **5** = 15 or **5** × **3** = 15
5. **11** × **4** = 44 or **4** × **11** = 44
6. **18** ÷ **3** = 6
7. 4 = **16** ÷ **4**
8. 45 = **9** × **5** or 45 = **5** × **9**
9. **8** × **3** = 24 or **3** × **8** = 24
10. 5 = **30** ÷ **6**

Page 55 — Mixed 3, 5 and 10 Times Tables
1. 3 × 5 = 20
2. 30 ÷ 10 = 5
3. 5 ÷ 50 = 10
4. 20 ÷ 5 = 2
5. 9 × 5 = 35
6. 30 ÷ 3 = 9

Page 56 — Mixed Times Tables
1. 1 × 5 — 6 ÷ 3
2. 12 ÷ 2 — 6 × 4
3. 2 × 10 — 100 ÷ 10
4. 2 × 5 — 30 ÷ 6
5. 24 ÷ 2 — 18 ÷ 3
6. 2 × 12 — 4 × 3
7. 4 × 4 — 8 × 2
8. 16 ÷ 8 — 5 × 4

Page 57 — Word Problems
1. 6 roses, 8 tulips
2. 12 roses, 16 tulips
3. 30 roses, 40 tulips
4. 15 roses, 20 tulips
5. 24 roses, 32 tulips
6. 27 roses, 36 tulips
7. 36 roses, 48 tulips